MAKE YOUR
Teddy Bears
& Bear Clothes

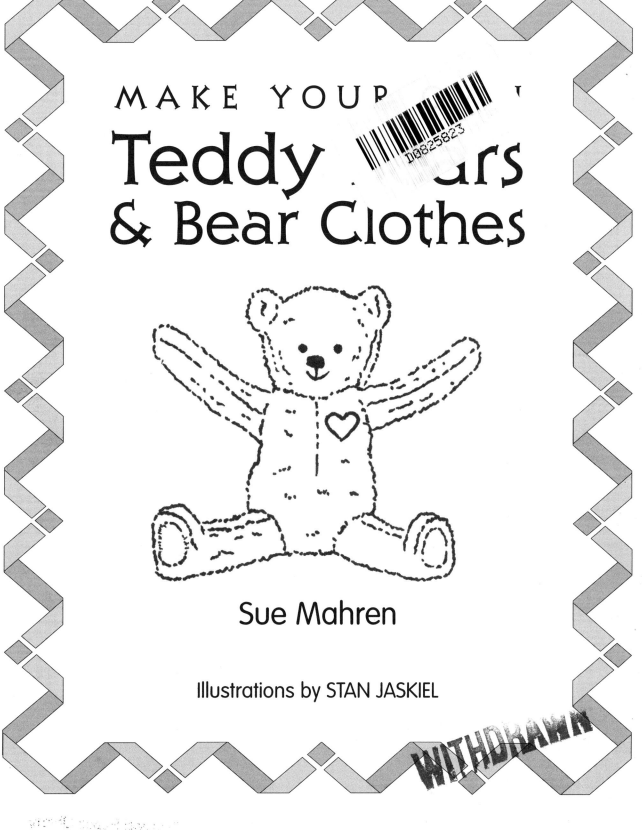

Sue Mahren

Illustrations by STAN JASKIEL

WILLIAMSON PUBLISHING ★ CHARLOTTE, VERMONT

Library of Congress Cataloging-in-Publication Data

Mahren, Sue.
    Make your own teddy bears & bear clothes! / Sue Mahren.
        p. cm. — (A Williamson quick starts for kids! book)
    Includes index.
    ISBN 1-885593-75-9 (pbk.)
    1. Soft toy making—Juvenile literature. 2. Teddy bears—Juvenile literature. 3. Doll clothes—Juvenile literature. [1. Toy making. 2. Sewing. 3. Teddy bears. 4. Handicraft.] I. Title. II. Series.

TT174.3 .M36 2000
745.592'43—dc21   00-047718

Quick Starts for Kids!™ series editor: **Susan Williamson**

Project editor: **Emily Stetson**

Illustrations: **Stan Jaskiel**

Interior design: **Bonnie Atwater**

Cover design: **Marie Ferrante-Doyle**

Cover illustrations: **Michael Kline**

Cover photography: **David A. Seaver**

Printing: **Capital City Press**

PERMISSIONS: Permission is granted by Williamson Publishing to adapt selected material from *Easy-to-Make Teddy Bears & All the Trimmings* by Jodie Davis. Clifford Berryman cartoon courtesy of Theodore Roosevelt Collection, Harvard College Library.

Williamson Publishing Co.
P.O. Box 185
Charlotte, VT 05445
(800) 234-8791

Manufactured in the United States of America

10 9 8 7 6 5 4 3 2 1

Little Hands®, Kids Can!®, Tales Alive!®, and *Kaleidoscope Kids®* are registered trademarks of Williamson Publishing.

Good Times™ and *Quick Starts for Kids!*™ are trademarks of Williamson Publishing.

NOTICE: The information contained in this book is true, complete, and accurate to the best of our knowledge. All recommendations and suggestions are made without any guarantees on the part of the author or Williamson Publishing. The author and publisher disclaim all liability incurred in conjunction with the use of this information.

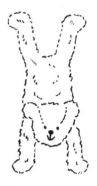

Dedication

To my children,

Sarah, Dylan, and Taylor,

who have always inspired

me and kept me young.

Contents

Create Your
Very Own Teddy!

If you've ever cuddled a soft, well-worn teddy bear, you know why of all stuffed toys, teddies are the favorites of kids and grown-ups of all ages. And you've likely run into Winnie-the-Pooh, Corduroy, or Paddington Bear somewhere in story land. Yes, it's clear: Teddy bears quickly find a special place in our hearts.

That was certainly true for me. I named my childhood teddy bear Benjamin. I took him everywhere — even on hiking and camping trips — and designed many outfits for him. With Benjamin by my side, I was never afraid of the dark, and together we had all sorts of adventures. Benjamin even went to college with me! (Really!)

Now, you can create and name your own special teddy. Yes, a teddy bear made *by you!* Everything you need to know to make and outfit a special teddy is right here, in these step-by-step directions. With your imagination and a few stitching supplies, you'll soon be a bear-making expert, cuddling a very special homemade teddy of your own!

Kids' Top 10 Bear-Making Questions ... With Answers!

1. *How big are the teddy bears?*

Little Bear is 6" (15 cm) tall, and Big Teddy is 16" (40 cm) tall — a perfect size for hugging!

2. *I've never sewn before, and I don't have a sewing machine. Can I still make a teddy bear and bear clothes?*

You bet! No sewing machine or fancy stitches are required. The bears and bear clothes you'll find here are specially designed for kids to make. Using patterns right from this book, you can trace onto the fabric, cut out the pieces, and then sew them together by hand. The Little Bear is an easy project to get you started, and each of the simple stitches is explained and illustrated so you can learn as you go. No sewing experience is needed!

3. *I don't have much money. How much is this going to cost?*

Homemade is best — and very inexpensive! You can make the *Quick Starts* 6" Little Bear with fabric scraps, and the 16" Big Teddy costs about $5 (it depends on the fabric and trimmings you choose).

4. *What if I get stuck? (No one in my family sews much.)*

Help is on the way! In fact, if you look at the how-to-do-it illustrations, you'll probably figure it out. If not, ask a teacher or the librarian or your next-door neighbor or your friend's mom. Lots of people sew, so keep asking. People who are good at figuring out puzzles are usually good at putting patterns together, so ask your math or graphic arts teachers, too.

5. *I don't know what a "seam allowance" is (Can I spend it?), and the other sewing words are all new to me, too. Does that matter?*

No problem! Any stitching words (such as "seam allowance") are explained in the text or on pages 59–62. In no time at all you'll be using sewing lingo like a pro! (By the way, you can't spend a seam allowance. It's just the amount of space you leave between the edge of the fabric and the stitching.)

6. *I like fuzzy bears. How will I know what fabric to use?*

Easy-to-use fabrics are suggested for each bear and for the bear clothes. (And to tell you the truth, it's tricky to sew with fake fur, so I've shared my secret solution for a soft, plush furlike fabric instead. It's called looped felt.)

7. *What other supplies do I need?*

Most of the pattern-making and sewing supplies are probably already around your house, but you can easily find what you need at a fabric or craft store. See the list on page 9 for details.

8. *How can I make my bear look the way I want it to?*

The fabric you choose, the amount of stuffing you use, and especially the expression on your bear's face will give character to your bear. Do you want a soft, cuddly bear, or one that's firm enough to stand up on its own? You decide!

9. *What should I dress my bear in?*

You know your bear best, so it's up to you! Make a wardrobe to go with each bear, using the clothes patterns on pages 34–58 to get started. Then, design some bear clothes and accessories of your own. It's easy to change the look: Just add trim to clothes or give your bear a hat, flowers, a ball and bat, a pair of glasses, a small pencil and pad of paper — anything that suits your bear.

10. *I have a lot of dolls. Can I use any of these designs for doll clothes, too?*

You sure can! Measure your dolls to see what size clothes you need and then increase or decrease the size of the patterns to make a doll wardrobe.

THE REAL STORY:

How the Teddy Bear Got Its Name

The political cartoon that started it all:
"DRAWING THE LINE IN MISSISSIPPI"
by Clifford Berryman

Have you ever heard of Theodore Roosevelt, the 26th president of the United States, who lived about 100 years ago? Well, Teddy Roosevelt (Teddy or Ted are nicknames for Theodore) loved nature and hunting. Once, when on a bear hunt in Mississippi with a group of people, the hunting guide still hadn't found any bears after three days. It looked as if the president's hunting trip would be a failure. The next day, the guide and his hunting dogs found a bear, but it was an old bear. Not wanting to disappoint the president, the guide followed it, and the dogs attacked and injured it. The guide tied the bear to a tree and called for the president.

When President Roosevelt saw the old, injured bear, he refused to shoot it, saying it was not fair to tie up an old bear to shoot for sport.

Some cartoonists heard about how the president had refused to shoot the bear and drew cartoons of President Theodore (Teddy) Roosevelt and the bear. Some showed a bear cub (rather than the old bear) shaking with fear. The cute bear-cub image became associated with the president. When a shopkeeper named two stuffed toy bears he had in his window "Teddy's Bears," the phrase "teddy bear" began to catch on. Today, every soft, cuddly toy bear is known as a teddy bear! And that's how teddy got its name!

The Bear Necessities

The most important bear-making tools are *your* creativity and *your* imagination. Really! So, begin by imagining what kind of bear you want, because that will guide you along the way. Of course, you'll need some fabric and matching thread to make the bear's body, plus some stuffing to fill it just right. But what else?

The box below lists the basic supplies you need to make a bear and bear outfits. But you won't need all of these items at once. *Check the materials listed at the beginning of each project to see what specific items you'll need.* I organize my supplies before I start cutting and sewing, just to be sure I have everything necessary for a particular project. That way, once I get started, I don't have to stop!

Basic Bear-Making Supplies

Things you probably have at home:

CEREAL-BOX CARDBOARD OR HEAVY PAPER — *for making sturdy patterns*

CHOPSTICK OR WOODEN SPOON — *for pushing the stuffing into the bear*

CRAFT SCISSORS — *for cutting paper and cardboard*

MASKING TAPE — *for holding fabric in place for sewing (if not using pins)*

MEASURING TAPE OR RULER — *for measuring fabric, ribbons, and elastic*

PENCIL — *for tracing book patterns onto tracing paper*

SEWING NEEDLES, SIZES 6–8 — *for hand sewing the bears and clothing*

STRAIGHT PINS — *to hold fabric or paper in place. Straight pins with a colored beaded top (called* quilting pins) *are easier to see.*

TRANSPARENT TAPE — *for taping pattern pieces together*

Things you may need to buy:

EMBROIDERY FLOSS, TWISTED-STRAND PEARL COTTON — *for embroidering eye, nose, and mouth details*

FABRIC — *for the bear's body and clothes*

FABRIC GLUE — *for gluing felt appliqués*

FABRIC SCISSORS (not the same as craft scissors), CHILD-SIZE — *for cutting fabric*

NEEDLE THREADER (optional) — *for extra-easy threading*

POLYESTER FIBERFILL — *for stuffing the bear*

QUILTER'S DISAPPEARING MARKING PEN — *for tracing cardboard patterns and transferring markings*

THIMBLE (OPTIONAL) — *for hand sewing, sized to fit your middle finger*

TRACING OR LIGHTWEIGHT TYPING PAPER — *for tracing patterns*

UPHOLSTERY OR QUILTING THREAD — *for sewing (it needs to be very strong!)*

... QUICK STARTS!

Sewing Tricks

🌀 **Big needle, strong thread!** Use a needle that is easy for you to thread. The higher the needle number size, the finer the needle; for bears and bear clothes, a medium size 6 to 8 needle is just right. You'll need strong *quilting* or *upholstery thread* to make strong stitches to hold your bear together for a long, long time.

🌀 **Need help threading your needle?** Needle threaders (found near the thread section in fabric stores) make it a cinch! (1) Push the wire end of the needle threader through the eye of your needle; (2) insert the thread through the wire of the threader; and (3) pull the wire back out of the needle. Now, remove the threader from the thread (4). Your needle is threaded!

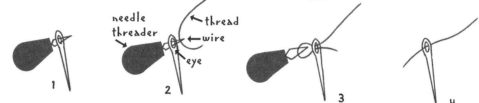

🌀 **Pins or tape?** Straight pins are great for holding fabric pieces together. The best straight pins for sewing bears and clothes (called *quilting pins*) have a colored beaded top that's easy to see. If you're sewing by hand, place the pins *parallel* to (in the same direction as) the seam you're sewing. If you're allowed to use a sewing machine, place the pins *perpendicular* to the seam (at a right angle — horizontal to the seam).

For simple seams, you can use a few pieces of masking tape to hold the fabric pieces together while you sew. Just tape over the edge of the seam, and then tear the tape off when you're done.

PIN PLACEMENT

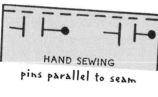

HAND SEWING
pins parallel to seam

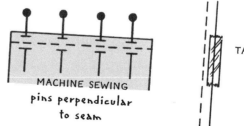

MACHINE SEWING
pins perpendicular
to seam

TAPE

🌀 **Be nimble and use a thimble.** Save those fingers! Use a thimble (that little "fingertip hat") on your middle finger. Poke the needle into the fabric, give it a push with the thimble, and out it comes on the other side, easy as pie! You can get kid-sized thimbles at a fabric store.

Who says a bear has to be furry? Old-fashioned bears were made with what-ever fabrics people had on hand. You can make a bear using felt, corduroy, or even a patchwork of cotton prints.

My favorite fabric for making a fuzzy-feel teddy is fuzzy looped felt. That's what I suggest you use for your first bear. The looped felt is soft and knobby on one side, giving a real furlike feel with a plush look; the reverse side is smooth, so it's easy to trace a pattern onto it. I buy looped felt in gray, beige, black, or brown colors from a craft store. And because it doesn't cost much to buy, I can use it to make all the bears I want!

BEAR BASICS

The Big Nap

No, this isn't about bear hibernation! NAP is the way the fur wants to lie naturally. To figure it out, just stroke the fur (or loops) as you would a dog's or cat's coat! You'll know when you go against the nap because the fuzz sticks up! When you place your patterns on the looped felt to cut them, make certain that all the pieces are positioned so they follow the same nap, indicated by the arrows on the patterns.

Making Little Bear!

This Little Bear is a snap to make — even if you've never sewn anything before. Create a Little Bear as a friend for your Big Teddy (page 19), or make several to give as gifts, to decorate a tree, to put on top of gift-wrapped packages, or to cheer someone up! I've also filled them with sprigs of lavender to make "beary nice" dream pillows.

Materials to make Little Bear:

Pattern-making supplies: pencil, tracing paper, craft scissors, cardboard or heavy paper, marking pen

Sewing supplies: fabric scissors, fabric glue, straight pins or masking tape, sewing needle

Cotton fabric: 7" x 14" (18 x 35 cm), solid or print, with matching thread

Chopstick or a pencil with an eraser (for pushing in the stuffing)

Polyester fiberfill

Ribbon, small piece

Embroidery floss, pearl-cotton type, optional (for eyes, nose, or mouth)

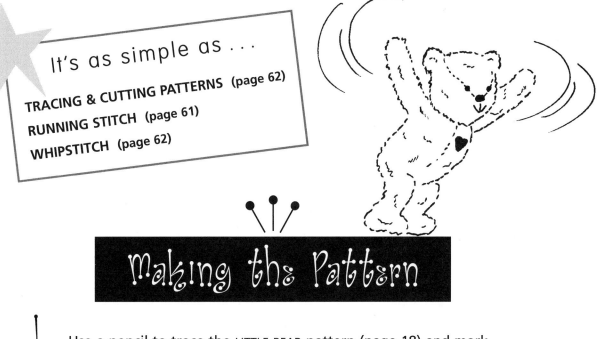

It's as simple as . . .

TRACING & CUTTING PATTERNS (page 62)

RUNNING STITCH (page 61)

WHIPSTITCH (page 62)

Making the Pattern

1. Use a pencil to trace the LITTLE BEAR pattern (page 18) and markings onto tracing paper.

2. Using craft scissors, cut out the pattern from the tracing paper. Place the pattern on cardboard and trace around it. Use a pencil to add the dots to the cardboard pattern.

3. Cut out the cardboard pattern and label it LITTLE BEAR (CUT 2).

1. Fold the fabric in half, with RIGHT SIDES TOGETHER (page 15). Pin the two pieces of fabric together to hold them in place.

2. Lay the pattern on the WRONG side (page 15) of the fabric. Trace around the pattern piece with a marking pen. Mark the two dots on the pattern onto *both* wrong sides of the fabric.

3. Use fabric scissors to cut along the traced lines, cutting out the two fabric bears.

FOLD

MARK DOTS

LITTLE BEAR CARDBOARD PATTERN

WRONG SIDE

RIGHT SIDES TOGETHER

SCRAPS!

Always place your pattern near the edge of the fabric to make your scraps as big as possible. And save those fabric scraps! You might want to use one to make the ears or foot pads of Big Teddy. So, keep a scrap bag handy.

Stitches, Lingo & How-To!

ALL STITCHES, LINGO, AND HOW-TO INSTRUCTIONS IN THIS BOOK ARE IN CAPITAL LETTERS AND ARE EXPLAINED WITH ILLUSTRATIONS IN THE TEXT OR IN THE *QUICK STARTS* ILLUSTRATED STITCH DICTIONARY & HOW-TO GUIDE ON PAGES 59–62.

How Can Fabric Be Wrong?

Every piece of fabric has two sides: a WRONG and a RIGHT. No, the fabric hasn't done anything good or bad. The *right* side looks like the finished material, such as the bright, printed side of a fabric or the fuzzy side of some looped felt. The *wrong* side is the faded side of the fabric or the backing, like the inside-out side of a shirt or dress.

When making bears and bear clothing, the cutting and sewing are usually done with the RIGHT SIDES TOGETHER, which means that they face against each other when your fabric is folded and look INSIDE OUT when you sew them together. This way, when you turn the stitched seams to the inside (so they won't show), the right sides face out — just the way you want them to! Another term you'll come across is RIGHT SIDE UP (the finished side of the fabric is facing up toward you).

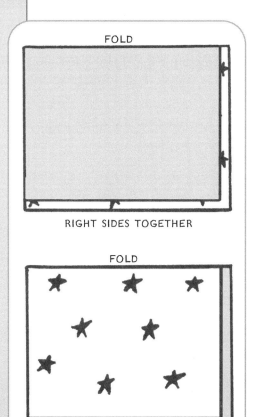

FOLD

RIGHT SIDES TOGETHER

FOLD

RIGHT SIDES OUT

··· *QUICK STARTS!*

Cut 2

When you fold the fabric, trace the pattern on top, and cut the pattern out, you end up with two matching fabric shapes because you're cutting through two layers of fabric in one cutting step!

Remember to use child-sized fabric scissors, not regular craft scissors, for cutting fabric. Fabric scissors are very sharp, so be extra careful. Never use fabric scissors for cutting paper. Paper will dull fabric scissors, and then they won't cut fabric!

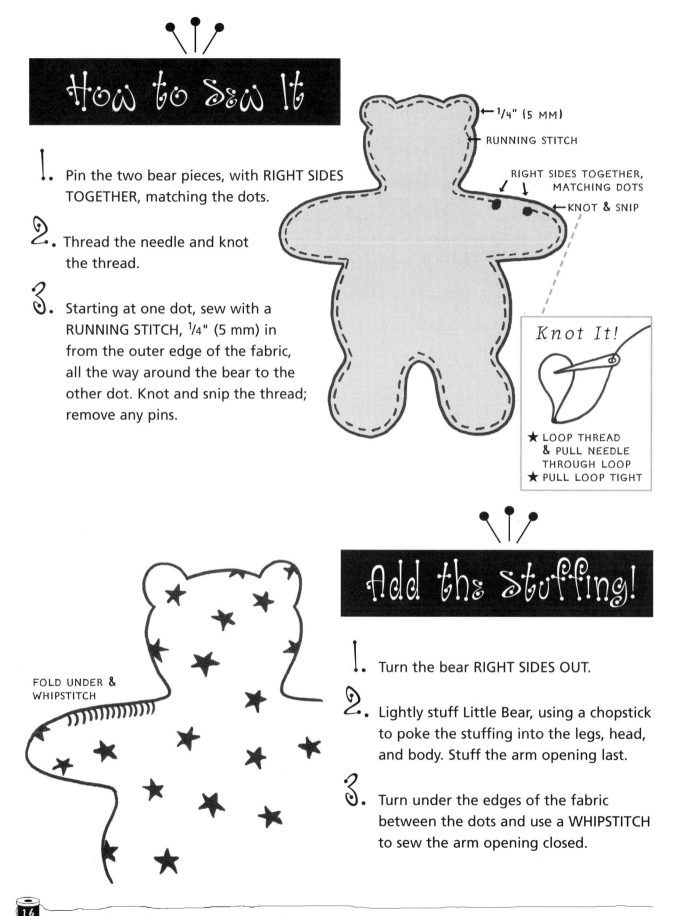

How to Sew It

1. Pin the two bear pieces, with RIGHT SIDES TOGETHER, matching the dots.

2. Thread the needle and knot the thread.

3. Starting at one dot, sew with a RUNNING STITCH, 1/4" (5 mm) in from the outer edge of the fabric, all the way around the bear to the other dot. Knot and snip the thread; remove any pins.

← 1/4" (5 MM)

← RUNNING STITCH

RIGHT SIDES TOGETHER, MATCHING DOTS

← KNOT & SNIP

Knot It!

★ LOOP THREAD & PULL NEEDLE THROUGH LOOP
★ PULL LOOP TIGHT

FOLD UNDER & WHIPSTITCH

Add the Stuffing!

1. Turn the bear RIGHT SIDES OUT.

2. Lightly stuff Little Bear, using a chopstick to poke the stuffing into the legs, head, and body. Stuff the arm opening last.

3. Turn under the edges of the fabric between the dots and use a WHIPSTITCH to sew the arm opening closed.

Stretch your creative muscles!

⊚ **Use furry felt or other fabrics** (page 11) for a different feel and look.

⊚ **Fill the bear with potpourri** rather than stuffing to make a teddy bear sachet.

⊚ **Use FRENCH KNOTS** (page 61) to make eyes or pretend buttons on your bear just before you stuff it. Or **add a heart-shaped felt APPLIQUÉ** (page 59) to your bear, using stitches or Velcro stick-on dots.

⊚ **Hang the bear as an ornament.** DOUBLE-THREAD (page 60) a needle with embroidery floss. Run it through the back of the head at the top, making a loop about 2" (5 cm) long. Knot and snip the thread.

Finishing Touches

🖐 Use a thin ribbon to tie a bow around the bear's neck.

🖐 Cut out and glue on a felt nose and mouth.

LITTLE BEAR
(CUT 2)

Make Your Own Teddy Bears

Making Big Teddy!

Lovable, huggable Big Teddy (16"/40 cm) is made in the same way as the Little Bear — by using a pattern and sewing by hand. Trace the pattern provided here onto the furry felt, cut the pieces out, sew them partially together, and then add the stuffing. It's that simple!

Materials to make Big Teddy:

Pattern-making supplies: pencil, tracing paper, craft scissors, cardboard or heavy paper, marking pen

Sewing supplies: fabric scissors, straight pins or masking tape, sewing needle

Looped felt fabric: ½ yard (18"/45 cm), with matching thread

Chopstick or a wooden spoon (for pushing in the stuffing)

Polyester fiberfill

Embroidery floss, pearl-cotton type, optional (for the eyes, nose, and mouth)

It's as simple as ...

TRACING & CUTTING PATTERNS
   (page 62)
RUNNING STITCH (page 61)
BACKSTITCH (page 59)
BASTING STITCH (page 60)
WHIPSTITCH (page 62)
SATIN STITCH (page 61)

CHECK IT OUT!

*O*ne of the biggest Oops! in sewing anything — and we all do it sometimes — is cutting something out the wrong way or not placing all the pieces on the fabric. I'm always really careful at this part of the bear-making process to be sure I know how many pieces of each pattern I'll need and which way they need to be cut.

Making the Patterns

Trace the Big Teddy patterns on pages 30–33 onto tracing paper with all the markings. Trace the paper patterns onto cardboard, transferring all of the markings. To make the HEAD GUSSET pattern, tape the HEAD GUSSET A and B patterns together before tracing onto cardboard. Cut out the cardboard pattern pieces and *label each one, marking how many of each you'll need to cut.*

Reversing Patterns

Looped felt is fairly thick, so it's best to cut through just one thickness of the fabric at a time. To get two pieces of the same pattern, you'll need to cut the fabric *twice* rather than cutting two pieces at once out of a double thickness of fabric (as you did when making Little Bear).

The pattern pieces are marked with instructions, such as "BIG TEDDY FRONT (CUT 2; 1 REVERSE)." This means that you cut two pieces total: Cut one front piece with the pattern as shown, and another one with the *pattern piece flipped over* (reversed), so that you have a right and a left front (page 22). To keep it simple, label one side of the *pattern* the REVERSE side when you are making the patterns.

··· QUICK STARTS!
Zip It Up!

Once you've made your patterns, you'll want to use them over and over again. To keep them together, store all pattern pieces for each bear or bear fashion in a large envelope or zip-locking bag. Mark the outside with the craft name (Big Teddy). Then, you can easily find the patterns to use next time!

Easy Layout and Cutting

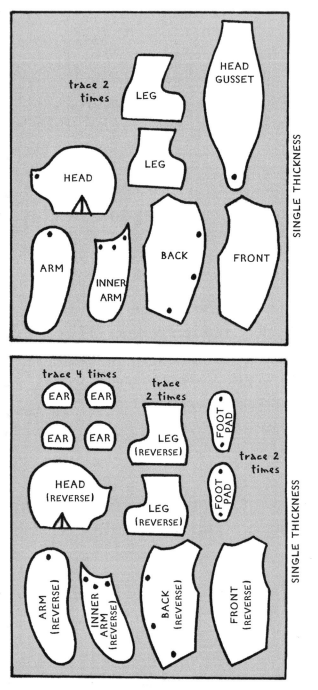

SINGLE THICKNESS

SINGLE THICKNESS

trace 2 times

LEG

HEAD GUSSET

LEG

HEAD

ARM

INNER ARM

BACK

FRONT

trace 4 times

EAR EAR

EAR EAR

trace 2 times

LEG (REVERSE)

FOOT PAD

HEAD (REVERSE)

LEG (REVERSE)

FOOT PAD

trace 2 times

ARM (REVERSE)

INNER ARM (REVERSE)

BACK (REVERSE)

FRONT (REVERSE)

1. Fold the fabric in half so you have two big rectangles. Cut it into two pieces along the fold.

2. Lay one fabric piece RIGHT SIDE DOWN, so the furry side is against your work surface and the woven backing is facing up. Lay out all the pattern pieces, following the arrows for the nap direction as marked, and use the marking pen to trace them onto the fabric. Trace a second LEG piece. Transfer any pattern markings on all patterns onto the fabric.

3. Lay the second fabric piece RIGHT SIDE DOWN. Flip over all the pattern pieces that need to be *reversed* and trace them onto the fabric, tracing the reversed LEG piece twice. Trace four EAR pieces and two FOOT PAD pieces. Transfer any pattern markings onto the fabric.

4. Use fabric scissors to cut out all the fabric pieces.

Sewing Piece by Piece

Front & Back

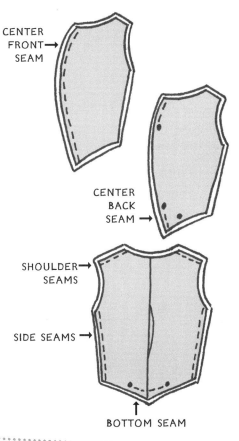

CENTER FRONT → SEAM

CENTER BACK SEAM →

SHOULDER → SEAMS

SIDE SEAMS →

↑ BOTTOM SEAM

1. Pin (or tape) the two FRONT pieces, RIGHT SIDES TOGETHER. Using a RUNNING STITCH, sew along the center front seam.

2. Pin the two BACK pieces, RIGHT SIDES TOGETHER, along the center back seam. Stitch from the top to the first dot, using a BACKSTITCH along the seam. Now BACKSTITCH from the second dot to the bottom.

3. Pin the FRONT to the BACK, RIGHT SIDES TOGETHER, matching left and right sides. Stitch the side and shoulder seams, and the bottom seam between the dots.

 ... *QUICK STARTS!*

Stitches & Seams

When sewing the bear parts, I made the seams ¼" (5 mm) in from the edge of the fabric, using the RUNNING STITCH. But if you find that it's difficult to use a running stitch through the fabric (because the fabric is so thick), sew one stitch at a time, going up and down with your needle instead of "running" along. It will take more time, but it may work better for you — and your bear!

If you find your running stitches are too far apart, try using the BACKSTITCH for all the seams. This strong stitch will hold your bear together for all your hugs.

By the way, that space between the edge of the fabric and the seam is called the SEAM ALLOWANCE.

Arms & Legs

1. Pin the ARMS to the INNER ARMS, RIGHT SIDES TOGETHER. Stitch, starting at one dot and going all the way around to the dot on the other side. Leave an opening at the top where the arm pieces overlap.

2. Match and pin two of the LEG pieces, RIGHT SIDES TOGETHER. Stitch the sides. Repeat for the second leg.

3. Pin a FOOT PAD to the bottom of each of the two LEGS, RIGHT SIDES TOGETHER, matching the dots to the leg seams. Stitch all the way around the FOOT PAD.

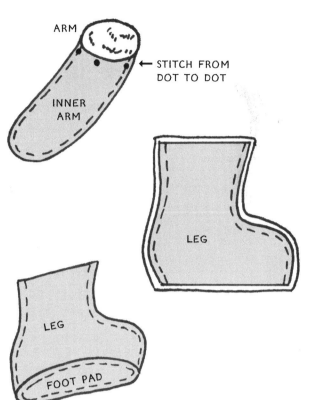

ARM

← STITCH FROM DOT TO DOT

INNER ARM

LEG

LEG

FOOT PAD

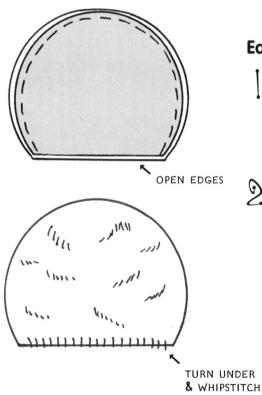

OPEN EDGES

TURN UNDER & WHIPSTITCH

Ears

1. Pin two EAR pieces, RIGHT SIDES TOGETHER. Stitch the rounded part, leaving the bottom edges open. Repeat for the other two EAR pieces.

2. Turn the ears RIGHT SIDES OUT. Turn under the bottom edges and WHIPSTITCH closed.

Head

1. Make DARTS in the two HEAD pieces.

2. Pin the two HEAD pieces, RIGHT SIDES TOGETHER, from the nose to the neck. Stitch.

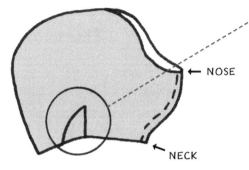

← NOSE

← NECK

A

FOLD OUT

KNOT AT TOP

B

FOLD

BACKSTITCH, STARTING AT WIDE EDGE

3. Pin the HEAD GUSSET to the two HEAD pieces, RIGHT SIDES TOGETHER. Start at the nose (**A**), then the sides (**B**), and then the top (**C**). Using the BASTING STITCH, sew to hold in place, and then stitch with a RUNNING STITCH.

C
TOP LAST

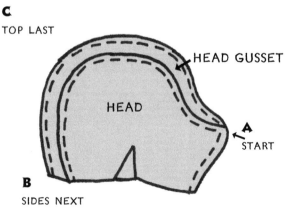

HEAD GUSSET

HEAD

A
START

B
SIDES NEXT

B E A R
B A S I C S

Darts: No Big Deal

A DART is simply a tuck in the fabric that makes the finished fabric curve — just what you need to make a round head for your bear! To make a dart, fold the fabric along the center line of the dart, RIGHT SIDES TOGETHER. Then, starting at the widest part of the dart, BACKSTITCH along the marked line to the tip.

Putting Teddy Together

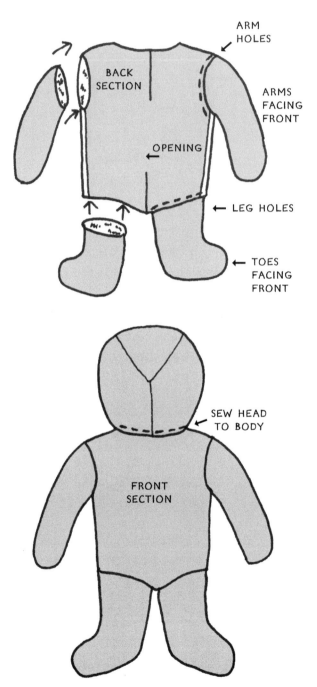

ARM HOLES

BACK SECTION

ARMS FACING FRONT

OPENING

← LEG HOLES

← TOES FACING FRONT

SEW HEAD TO BODY

FRONT SECTION

1. With the bear's body and legs still INSIDE OUT, pin the LEGS to the LEG HOLES. Be sure the legs and toes are facing toward the front section of the body. Match the arm dots to the side seams and BASTE together. Then, remove the pins and BACKSTITCH or WHIPSTITCH the seams to make them strong so your bear stays together!

2. Pin the INSIDE OUT ARMS to the ARM HOLES, matching the dots and seams. Make sure the arms face toward the front section of the body. BASTE and then BACKSTITCH or WHIPSTITCH.

3. Pin the INSIDE OUT HEAD to the INSIDE OUT BODY, matching the seams and dots. BASTE and then BACKSTITCH or WHIPSTITCH.

4. Turn the bear RIGHT SIDES OUT. All the parts should be pointing in the right directions. Now you're ready to stuff your bear!

STEP 5
The Right Stuff

Congratulations! You've fashioned Big Teddy's arms, legs, body, and head; now it's time to start stuffing! This is where you give Big Teddy that soft, huggable quality.

- Good-quality polyester fiberfill is most often used to stuff bears — it's safe to use and won't cause allergies.

- Stuff the hard-to-reach parts (head, arms, and legs) before you stuff the body.

- Stuff the paws and feet so they feel hard and then lighten up as you move up the limb.

- Test huggability: Give each limb a squeeze!

- Stuff fabric scraps into the body of the bear for future emergency repairs. That way, you'll always have matching fabric available.

- When you think Big Teddy has the right feel, turn under the rough edges of the back opening, pin it closed, and WHIPSTITCH to secure the seam.

TURN UNDER EDGES & WHIPSTITCH

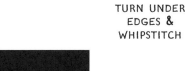

STEP 6
Designing Teddy's Face

Give Big Teddy some personality ... with a face that's as unique as yours! Experiment to find the look you like most.

You can ...

★ Move pins around to test a design, using larger or smaller pin ends for pretend eyes and a nose.

★ Change the size, color, and placement of the eyes.

★ Change the nose shape or the slant or shape of the mouth.

★ Move the ears closer together or farther apart.

To add ears:

1. Decide where you want the ears to go. Mark the placement with a pin; then, use heavy thread or embroidery floss to WHIPSTITCH the EARS to the HEAD.

2. Knot the thread and cut off the excess.

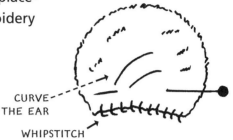

CURVE THE EAR

WHIPSTITCH

... *QUICK STARTS!*

The Scoop on Ears

Want to know how teddy bears get a slightly cupped shape to their ears? Push a pin through one side of the bottom edge of the ear and back out the other side of the ear. Do you see the bend you made in the ear? After you stitch the ear to the head, remove the pin.

To add embroidered eyes:

1. After you've stuffed the bear's head, use a pencil to sketch eye patterns on tracing paper. When you find one you like, use a marking pen to trace the shapes for the eyes onto regular felt and glue or pin them in place on the bear.

2. With matching pearl-cotton embroidery floss, sew a SATIN STITCH over the felt. Keep your stitches very close together to make a solid eye.

3 FELT EYES

To make a foolproof mouth and nose:

1. Use a pencil to trace a nose and mouth pattern onto tracing paper. Using a marking pen, trace the pattern onto regular felt (choose a different color from your bear's body color).

2. Cut out the felt with fabric scissors and glue it in place.

3. With matching pearl-cotton embroidery floss, sew with a SATIN STITCH across the nose.

4. When you reach the end of the nose, bring the needle up just under the nose, in the center, and follow the pattern for the mouth.

5. Fasten the thread with a tiny knot under the nose. Clip the thread close to the fabric.

B E A R
B A S I C S

Embroider with Pearls

Pearl cotton, that is! This type of embroidery floss is twisted around itself so it doesn't separate into individual strands the way regular floss does. It's much easier to work with!

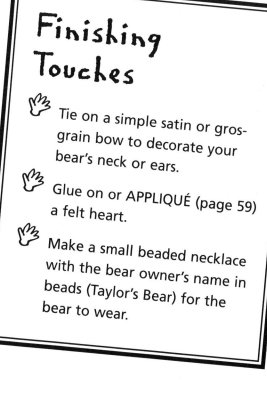

Finishing Touches

- Tie on a simple satin or gros-grain bow to decorate your bear's neck or ears.

- Glue on or APPLIQUÉ (page 59) a felt heart.

- Make a small beaded necklace with the bear owner's name in beads (Taylor's Bear) for the bear to wear.

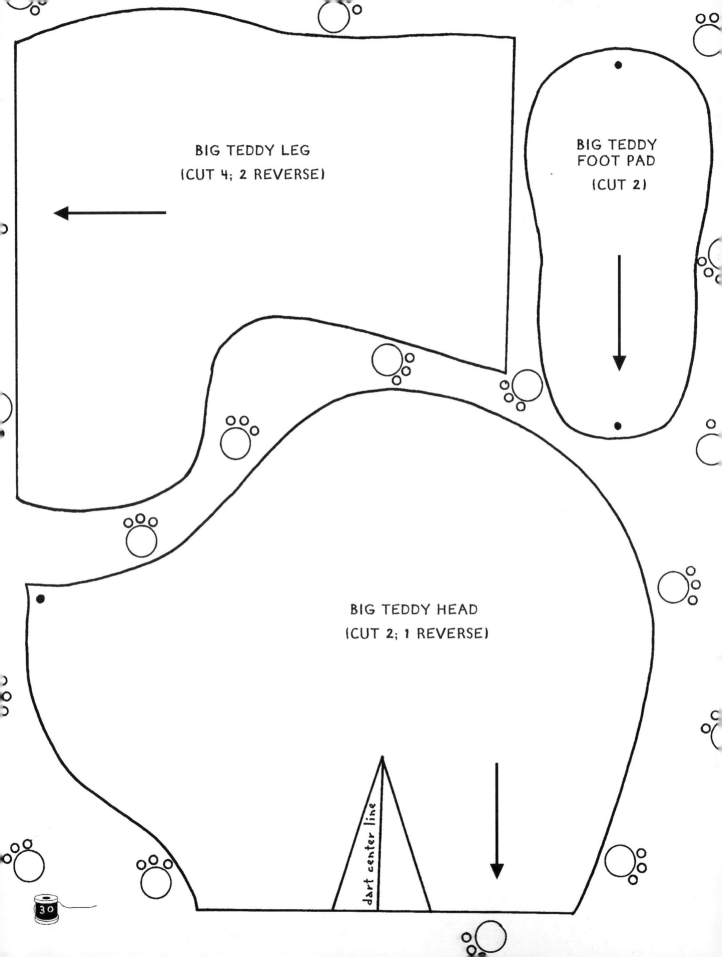

BIG TEDDY LEG
(CUT 4; 2 REVERSE)

BIG TEDDY
FOOT PAD
(CUT 2)

BIG TEDDY HEAD
(CUT 2; 1 REVERSE)

dart center line

30

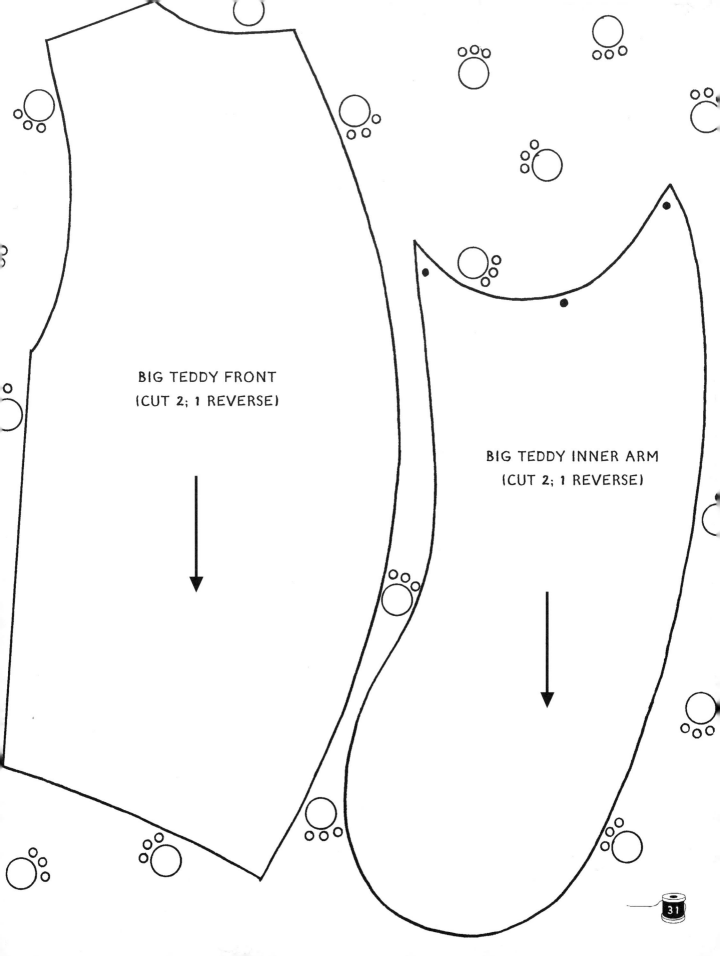

BIG TEDDY FRONT
(CUT 2; 1 REVERSE)

BIG TEDDY INNER ARM
(CUT 2; 1 REVERSE)

31

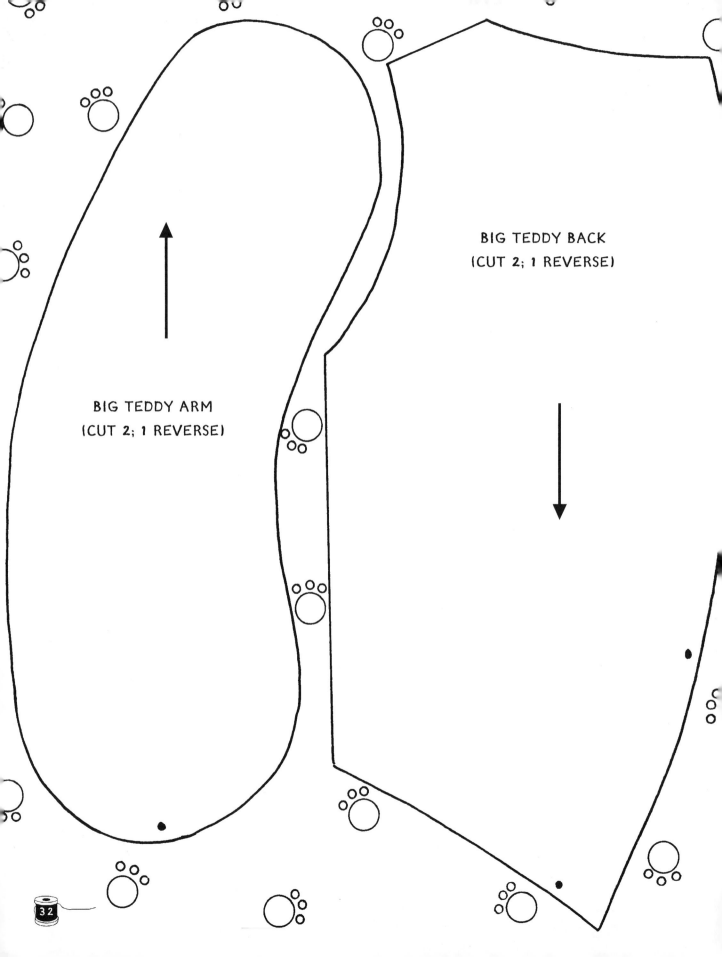

BIG TEDDY ARM
(CUT 2; 1 REVERSE)

BIG TEDDY BACK
(CUT 2; 1 REVERSE)

32

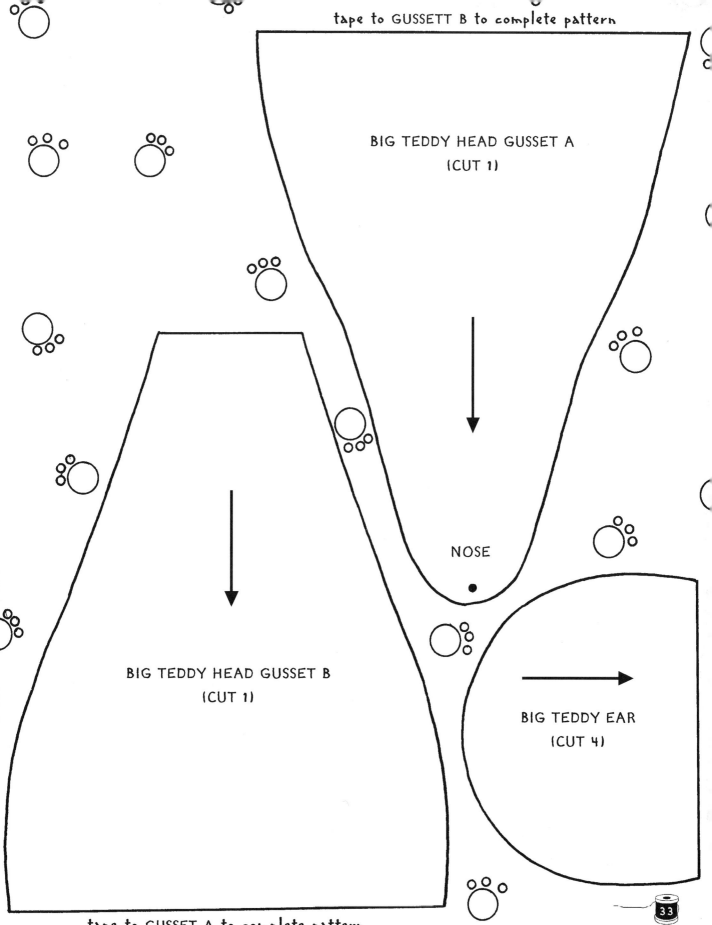

tape to GUSSETT B to complete pattern

BIG TEDDY HEAD GUSSET A
(CUT 1)

BIG TEDDY HEAD GUSSET B
(CUT 1)

NOSE

BIG TEDDY EAR
(CUT 4)

tape to GUSSET A to complete pattern

Bear Fashions

You can create an entire wardrobe for your bear using the simple patterns found here. Begin with an easy, no-sew shawl or scarf, or an apron or cape, and then fashion a skirt or pair of pants, a fun cap, or a fancy vest. You can even make a pair of boots for Big Teddy's feet! Once you enter the world of bear fashions, you'll be able to create clothes of your own design for your bears!

Mix and match outfits and add your own trimmings. I like to use brightly patterned cottons, soft flannel, denim, and felt to give my bears a lot of variety. Whatever suits *your* style is the *right* style for suiting up Big Teddy!

The Quick Starts Guide™ to FAST FASHIONS!

... QUICK STARTS!
Two-for-One Outfits

Here's an idea that let's you make two outfits in the time it takes to make just one! Pick out two different fabric types, colors, or prints, and cut out the pieces for both outfits at the same time. Then, complete each sewing step for both materials as you go. This "assembly line" sewing will save you time!

NOTE: *For each outfit, patterns are sized to fit a 16" (40 cm) teddy bear.*

Stitches, Lingo & How-To!

ALL STITCHES, LINGO, AND HOW-TO INSTRUCTIONS IN THIS BOOK ARE IN CAPITAL LETTERS AND ARE EXPLAINED WITH ILLUSTRATIONS IN THE TEXT OR IN THE *QUICK STARTS* ILLUSTRATED STITCH DICTIONARY & HOW-TO GUIDE ON PAGES 59–62.

No-Sew Shawl and Neck Scarf

No patterns or sewing needed! Here's a great way to use larger scraps.

Materials to make a shawl and scarf:

Measuring tape

Fabric scissors

For shawl: wool, flannel, or cotton print fabric, 18" x 18" (45 x 45 cm)

For scarf: wool, flannel, or cotton print fabric, 3" x 18" (7.5 x 45 cm)

Sewing needle

Safety pin or self-sticking Velcro dots (shawl only)

Make the Fringe

1. To create fringe, use a sewing needle to pull out the threads along the edges.

2. Fold and wrap the shawl around the bear's shoulders. Secure with a small safety pin or self-sticking Velcro dots. Wrap scarf around bear's head.

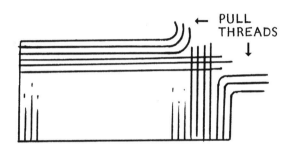

PULL THREADS

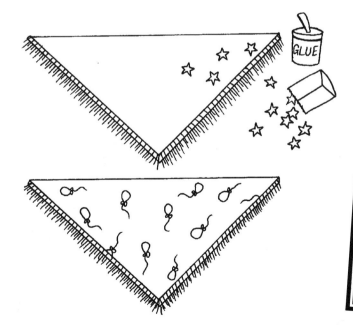

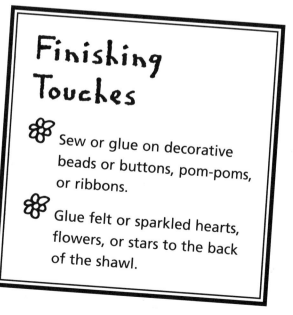

Finishing Touches

❀ Sew or glue on decorative beads or buttons, pom-poms, or ribbons.

❀ Glue felt or sparkled hearts, flowers, or stars to the back of the shawl.

No-Sew Stocking Cap

No pattern or sewing needed!

Materials to make a stocking cap:

Fabric scissors
Old, clean sock (adult size works best)

Cut & Shape

1. Using fabric scissors, cut off the sock's toe.
2. Let the toe's cut edge roll up. No need to hem it!

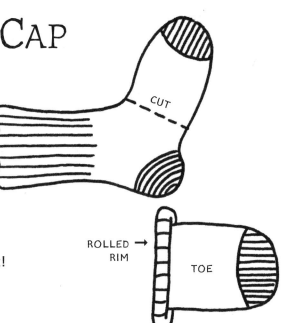

Straw Hat

Outfit Big Teddy for a day in the sun! Choose a simple straw hat, available from craft shops, add 1 yard (1 m) of ½" (1 cm) width ribbon, and decorate it with your own trimmings!

1. Wrap the ribbon around the hat one and a half times. Glue the ribbon in place all the way around the hat, tucking the ends in.
2. Staple on an elastic tie to hold the hat under your bear's chin.

QUICK STARTS APRON

No pattern needed!

Materials to make an apron:

Sewing supplies: fabric scissors, straight pins or masking tape, measuring tape, sewing needle, safety pin

Eyelet lace fabric: 8" x 10" (20 x 25 cm), with matching thread

Ribbon: 1 yard (1 m) of ¾" (2 cm) width

It's as simple as ...
RUNNING STITCH (page 61)

Case & Sew!

1. Position the lace fabric as shown, with the long sides on top and bottom.

2. To make the *casing* (or fabric "tunnel") for the ribbon, fold over the top edge of the lace 1" (2.5 cm). Pin and stitch the lower edge of the fold, using a RUNNING STITCH. (Make sure to leave a space for the ribbon between your stitches and the fold.) Leave both ends open to insert the ribbon.

3. Attach a safety pin to one end of the ribbon. Guide the pin through one opening of the casing all the way out the other side.

4. Tie the apron around the bear's waist. When you have it gathered (bunched) the way you like, make a couple of stitches on each side so the ribbon stays put. Trim the ends of the ribbon as needed.

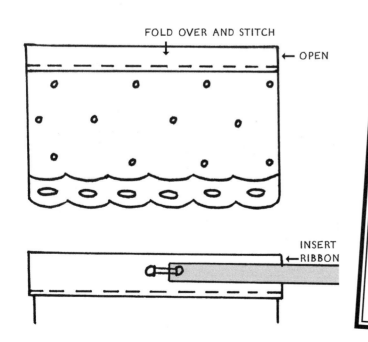

FOLD OVER AND STITCH

← OPEN

INSERT
← RIBBON

Finishing Touches

❀ Mix and match. Make scarves, shawls, aprons, and stocking caps from several different fabrics so that you'll have different styles.

❀ Sew or glue several rows of ric-rac (a decorative trim) to the bottom of the apron.

COOL CAPE

This cape is so easy to make, you'll want several in different colors. It will keep Big Teddy warm on winter days or shed the rain during spring showers.

It's as simple as ...

TRACING AND CUTTING PATTERNS (page 62)

RUNNING STITCH (page 61)

WHIPSTITCH (page 62)

Materials to make a cape:

Pattern-making supplies: pencil, tracing paper, craft scissors, marking pen, cardboard or heavy paper

Sewing supplies: fabric scissors, straight pins or masking tape, sewing needle

Felt fabric: 14" x 28" (35 x 70 cm), with matching thread

Ribbon: 1/4" (5 mm) width

For hat, see page 44.

From Pattern to Fabric

1. Use a pencil to trace the CAPE FRONT and CAPE BACK patterns on page 51 onto the tracing paper. Mark the dots.

2. Cut out the paper patterns and trace them onto cardboard. Cut out the patterns; then, label and mark the dots.

3. Fold the fabric in half, with RIGHT SIDES TOGETHER. Pin together to hold in place. Place the CAPE BACK pattern against the fold. Place the CAPE FRONT piece next to it. Trace and cut out the fabric pieces, but don't cut along the CAPE BACK fold.

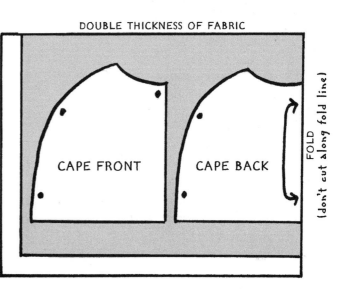

DOUBLE THICKNESS OF FABRIC

CAPE FRONT   CAPE BACK

FOLD (don't cut along fold line)

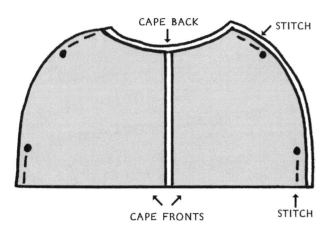

CAPE BACK

STITCH

CAPE FRONTS

STITCH

Making the Cape

1. Pin the two CAPE FRONT pieces to the CAPE BACK piece, with RIGHT SIDES TOGETHER. Use a RUNNING STITCH to sew from the neck to the top of the arm opening and then from the bottom of the arm opening to the hem. Repeat for the other side. Turn the cape RIGHT SIDES OUT.

2. Cut the ribbon to make two ties long enough to tie a bow at the neck of the cape. WHIPSTITCH the pieces of ribbon in place at the front edges (see finished cape on page 39).

Stretch your creative muscles!

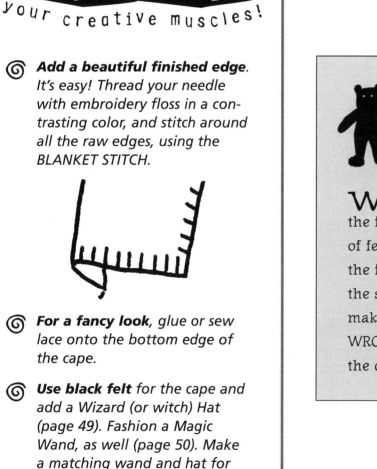

🌀 **Add a beautiful finished edge.** *It's easy! Thread your needle with embroidery floss in a contrasting color, and stitch around all the raw edges, using the BLANKET STITCH.*

🌀 **For a fancy look,** *glue or sew lace onto the bottom edge of the cape.*

🌀 **Use black felt** *for the cape and add a Wizard (or witch) Hat (page 49). Fashion a Magic Wand, as well (page 50). Make a matching wand and hat for yourself!*

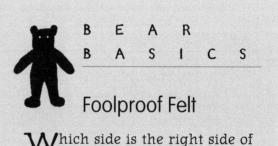

BEAR BASICS

Foolproof Felt

Which side is the right side of the felt? Either side! The beauty of felt is that either side can be the finished side — they both look the same! But you'll still need to make one side the inside or WRONG SIDE of the cape and one the outside, or RIGHT SIDE.

SIMPLE SKIRT & PERFECTLY EASY PANTS

Make a skirt or pants, using a fabric of your choice.

It's as simple as ...

TRACING & CUTTING PATTERNS (page 62)

RUNNING STITCH (page 61)

TOPSTITCH (page 62)

Materials to make a skirt or pants:

Pattern-making supplies: pencil, tracing paper, ruler, craft scissors, marking pen, cardboard or heavy paper

Sewing supplies: measuring tape, fabric scissors, straight pins or masking tape, sewing needle, safety pin

Flannel fabric: 1/3 yard (30 cm) per pair of pants or skirt, with matching thread

Elastic: 14" (35 cm) of 1/4" or 1/2" (5 mm to 1 cm) width

Embroidery floss, pearl-cotton type (for topstitching)

Making the Patterns

Use a pencil to trace the PANTS pattern on page 52 onto tracing paper. Cut out the pattern and trace it onto cardboard. To make the SKIRT pattern, draw a 6" x 10" (15 x 25 cm) rectangle onto cardboard. Cut out and label the cardboard patterns.

... *QUICK STARTS!*

"Seams" So Easy!

All SEAM ALLOWANCES on the Bear Fashions are 1/4" (5 mm) unless noted otherwise. That means you can sew close to the edge of the fabric, and you won't have to iron the finished seams!

Fabric: Fold, then Cut

1. Fold the fabric in half, with RIGHT SIDES TOGETHER.

2. *To make the skirt:* Place the short edge of the SKIRT pattern against the fold line, but don't cut along the fold (you'll end up with one long piece).

3. *To make the pants:* Place the PANTS pattern down twice so you'll end up with four pieces. *Once you're satisfied all the pieces will fit,* trace around each pattern piece with a fabric marker.

4. Use fabric scissors to cut out the pieces.

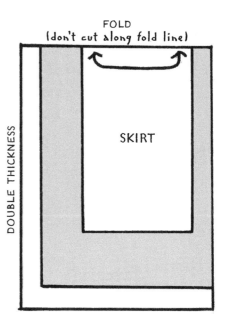

FOLD
(don't cut along fold line)

DOUBLE THICKNESS

SKIRT

CHECK IT TWICE!

Remember the problem of cutting mistakes (page 20)? If you cut something out incorrectly, you'll need to start over, so please take your time here, checking the layout and making sure all the needed pieces fit before tracing and cutting! Remember not to cut along the fold line. This part can get kind of tricky.

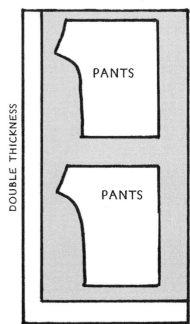

DOUBLE THICKNESS

PANTS

PANTS

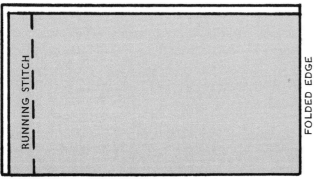

RUNNING STITCH

FOLDED EDGE

DOUBLE THICKNESS

Making the Skirt

1. Match the short edges of the SKIRT, with RIGHT SIDES TOGETHER. Pin in place.

2. Use the RUNNING STITCH to sew the edges together.

3. After you've made your seams, FINGER-PRESS them flat.

Making the Pants

1. With the fabric RIGHT SIDES TOGETHER, pin and sew the short inner seam of the two PANTS pieces, using a RUNNING STITCH. FINGER-PRESS the seam open. Repeat for the other two PANTS pieces.

2. Pin the front and back of the pants, RIGHT SIDES TOGETHER. Sew the long, curved crotch seams, matching the short inside seams. CLIP THE CURVES.

3. Pin and stitch the two side seams.

Casing the Waist

1. To make the *casing* (or fabric "tunnel") for the elastic, fold over the top edge of the fabric 1" (2.5 cm). Pin and stitch the lower edge (see below), using a RUNNING STITCH. Be sure to leave a 1" (2.5 cm) opening in the stitching — this is where you'll insert the elastic.

2. Attach a safety pin to one end of the elastic. Guide the pin through the opening and all the way around.

3. Pin the two ends of elastic together at the opening. Try the skirt or pants on the bear. Adjust the elastic as needed; then, overlap the edges of elastic and stitch together.

STITCH

[STEP 1]

FINGER-PRESS SEAM FLAT & MATCH TO OTHER SEAM

SIDE SEAM

[STEP 2]

CROTCH SEAM

Stretch your creative muscles!

- **Make knickers.** *Cut the bottoms of the pants a little shorter; then, TOPSTITCH a hem.*

- **Use a contrasting color** *of embroidery floss for your stitching. It will make the hem and casing really stand out!*

- **Add a hat.** *Top off the skirt or pants with a designed-by-you Straw Hat (page 37) or Easy Fun Hat (page 44).*

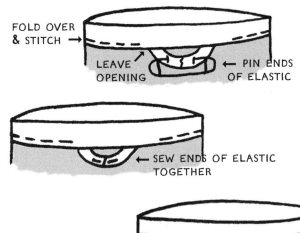

FOLD OVER & STITCH

LEAVE OPENING

PIN ENDS OF ELASTIC

SEW ENDS OF ELASTIC TOGETHER

Hemming

1. To make a hem, fold the fabric on the bottom of the pants or the skirt up 1/2" (1 cm). TOPSTITCH.

2. Turn the skirt or pants RIGHT SIDES OUT.

EASY FUN HAT

Give Big Teddy a stylish look in a custom-made hat! You can even choose two different colors of felt — one for the top and one for the body. Then, choose a different color of embroidery floss to make the final stitching really stand out!

Materials to make a hat:

Pattern-making supplies: pencil, tracing paper, ruler, craft scissors, marking pen, cardboard or heavy paper

Sewing supplies: fabric scissors, straight pins or masking tape, sewing needle, contrasting thread

Felt fabric: 12" x 22" (30 x 55 cm)

Embroidery floss, pearl-cotton type (optional)

It's as simple as ...

TRACING & CUTTING PATTERNS (page 62)

RUNNING STITCH (page 61)

BASTING STITCH (page 60)

BLANKET STITCH (page 60)

From Pattern to Fabric

1. Trace the HAT TOP pattern from page 53 onto tracing paper. Cut out the paper pattern and trace it onto cardboard. To make the HAT BODY pattern, draw a 4" x 10" (10 x 25 cm) rectangle. Cut out and label the cardboard patterns.

2. Fold the fabric in half, with RIGHT SIDES TOGETHER. Pin the two pieces together to hold. Place the short end of the HAT BODY pattern on the wrong side of the fabric against the fold as shown. Trace and cut out the BODY piece. (Don't cut along the fold.) Unfold the fabric and cut the HAT TOP from the single thickness of fabric.

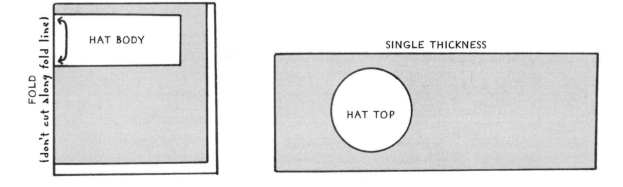

DOUBLE THICKNESS

HAT BODY

FOLD (don't cut along fold line)

SINGLE THICKNESS

HAT TOP

Put It Together!

1. Using a RUNNING STITCH, sew the back seam of the BODY, with RIGHT SIDES TOGETHER. FINGER-PRESS the seam flat.

2. With RIGHT SIDES TOGETHER, pin the TOP to the BODY. BASTE; then, stitch along the bottom edge with a RUNNING STITCH to hold.

3. Turn the hat RIGHT SIDES OUT. Add BLANKET STITCHING or TOPSTITCHING along the bottom edge, using embroidery floss. Turn up the edge for a finished look.

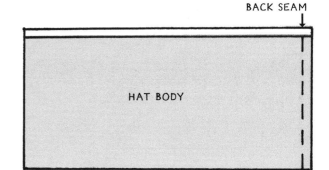

BACK SEAM

HAT BODY

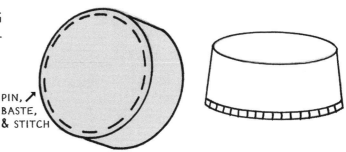

PIN, ↗
BASTE,
& STITCH

S·t·r·e·t·c·h
your creative muscles!

Making a Reversible Easy Fun Hat

1. *Follow the directions for the Easy Fun Hat, but cut two pieces of each pattern — one from a cotton print and one from a contrasting cotton print. You'll end up with four fabric pieces in all (two TOPS and two BODY pieces).*

2. *Sew the back seam of each BODY piece. Then, pin and sew each BODY to a* contrasting TOP piece. You'll have two separate hats.

3. *Fitting one hat inside the other (**A**), pin your two hats together along the bottom edge, with RIGHT SIDES TOGETHER.*

4. *Sew a RUNNING STITCH along the bottom edge, leaving a small opening (**B**).*

5. *Turn the hat RIGHT SIDES OUT. Fold over the open edge and WHIPSTITCH it closed. TOPSTITCH the bottom edge if desired (**C**).*

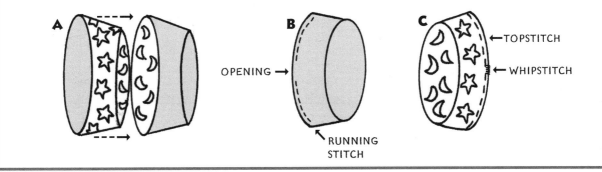

A

B

OPENING →

C

←TOPSTITCH

← WHIPSTITCH

↖ RUNNING STITCH

QUICK STARTS EASY FELT VEST

With felt, you don't need to reverse any pattern pieces, and there are only two seams to sew! This vest can be done in a flash.

It's as simple as ...

TRACING & CUTTING PATTERNS (page 62)

RUNNING STITCH (page 61)

Materials to make a felt vest:

Pattern-making supplies: pencil, tracing paper, craft scissors, marking pen, cardboard or heavy paper

Sewing supplies: measuring tape, fabric scissors, masking tape or straight pins, sewing needle, safety pin

Felt fabric: 12" x 12" (30 x 30 cm)

Embroidery floss (of a contrasting color)

Trace & Cut

1. Trace the VEST BACK and VEST FRONT patterns on pages 54–55 onto tracing paper. Cut out the paper patterns and trace them onto cardboard. Cut out and label the cardboard patterns.

2. Fold the felt in half. Place the patterns as shown. Trace, mark, and cut out the felt pieces. Do not cut along the fold.

DOUBLE THICKNESS

FOLD
(don't cut along fold line)

VEST BACK

VEST FRONT

Sewing the Seams

Pin the VEST BACK and VEST FRONTS to each other. Sew the shoulder seams and side seams, using a RUNNING STITCH. FINGER-PRESS the seams flat. Turn the rough seams to the inside.

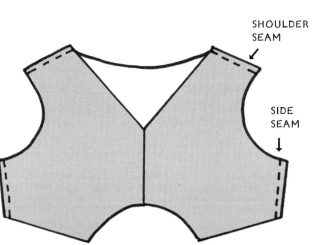

SHOULDER SEAM

SIDE SEAM

Finishing Touches

- 🖐 To add a decorative look, sew a BLANKET STITCH in a contrasting color along the edges of the vest, APPLIQUÉ felt designs, or use FRENCH KNOTS (page 61) to attach stars or buttons onto the front and back sections.

- 🖐 Try several colors of felt — maybe one for the back and two different colors for the two front pieces.

SNAZZY FELT BOOTS

These simple boots are made out of felt for extra-easy assembly. Make several pairs of different colors to match Big Teddy's outfits!

It's as simple as ...
TRACING & CUTTING PATTERNS (page 62)
BLANKET STITCH (page 60)

Materials to make a pair of boots:

Pattern-making supplies: pencil, tracing paper, craft scissors, marking pen, cardboard or heavy paper

Sewing supplies: fabric scissors, straight pins or masking tape, sewing needle

Felt fabric: 2 pre-cut 8½" x 11" (22 x 28 cm) sections

Embroidery floss, pearl-cotton type, in a contrasting color

2 small bells (optional)

 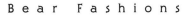

Making the Boot

1. Trace the BOOT and BOOT BOTTOM patterns from page 56 onto tracing paper. Cut out the paper patterns and trace them onto cardboard. Cut out and label the cardboard patterns.

2. Fold the felt in half. Trace the patterns onto the felt and cut the pieces out. Remember to cut four BOOT pieces. There's no need to reverse the patterns because both sides of the felt are the same.

3. Pin two of the BOOT sides together. Using the BLANKET STITCH, sew the sides, leaving the bottom and top open. Repeat for the other boot.

4. Pin a BOOT BOTTOM to the sides of one boot. Sew with a BLANKET STITCH. Repeat for the other boot.

5. Trim out the top of each boot with the BLANKET STITCH. Turn down the cuff.

6. Sew a bell on the tip of each toe.

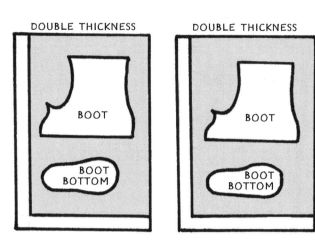

DOUBLE THICKNESS   DOUBLE THICKNESS

BOOT   BOOT

BOOT BOTTOM   BOOT BOTTOM

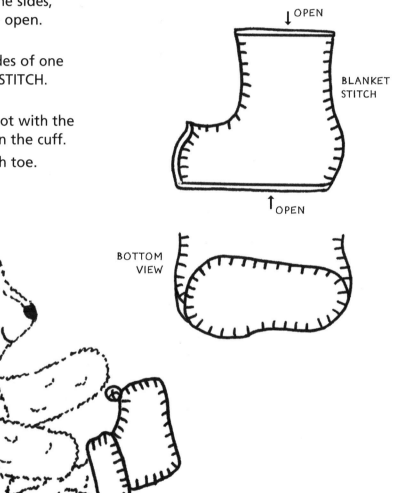

OPEN

BLANKET STITCH

OPEN

BOTTOM VIEW

BEAR WIZARD HAT & MAGIC WAND

This wizard hat is so much fun to make and wear, you'll want to make one for yourself! Contrasting felt colors give the hat even more pizzazz, and you can appliqué star, sun, and moon shapes for a really special design.

Materials to make a wizard hat:

Pattern-making supplies: pencil, tracing paper, craft scissors, marking pen, cardboard or heavy paper

Sewing supplies: fabric scissors, straight pins or masking tape, sewing needle

Felt fabric: 2 precut 8 ½" x 11" (22 x 28 cm)

Embroidery floss, pearl-cotton type, (of a contrasting color)

Small bell or sequin star (one per hat)

It's as simple as ...
TRACING & CUTTING PATTERNS (page 62)
BLANKET STITCH (page 60)

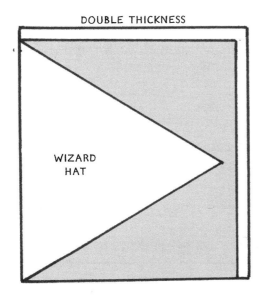

DOUBLE THICKNESS

WIZARD HAT

Making the Hat

1. Trace the WIZARD HAT pattern from page 57 onto tracing paper. Cut out the paper pattern and trace onto cardboard. Cut out and label the cardboard pattern.

2. Stack the felt pieces together. For a two-colored hat, use two different colors of felt. Trace the pattern onto the felt and cut the pieces out.

3. Pin the felt together at the sides and sew, using a BLANKET STITCH. Leave an opening at the bottom for the head.

4. Open the hat and decorate the bottom edge with a BLANKET STITCH.

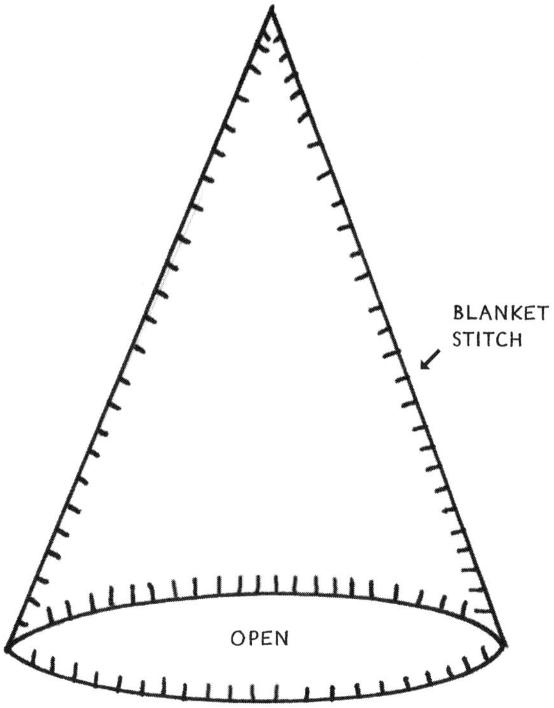

Finishing Touches

✋ Sew on a bell or a sequin star at the top of the hat.

✋ APPLIQUÉ a felt moon, sun, or star to the side of the hat (page 58).

BLANKET STITCH

OPEN

MAGIC WAND

Materials to make a wand:

Pencil and tracing paper
Foil paper (available from art and crafts stores)
Scissors
Glue
1/4" (5 mm) wooden dowel:
6" (15 cm) for the bear wand and
12" (30 cm) for a child-sized wand
Sandpaper
Tempera paint and paintbrush
* Hot-glue gun (set on low)
Glitter

Please ask a grown-up to help you. These can get very hot.

Make the Star

1. Trace the WAND STAR pattern from page 58 onto tracing paper. Cut out the paper pattern and trace it twice onto the foil paper. Cut out the foil stars.

2. Glue the stars together, with the shiny side facing out.

Make the Wand

1. Sand the ends of the wooden dowel. Paint the wand with tempera paints and let dry.

2. With grown-up help, hot-glue the star to the dowel.

3. Add glitter to the wand and star for extra sparkle.

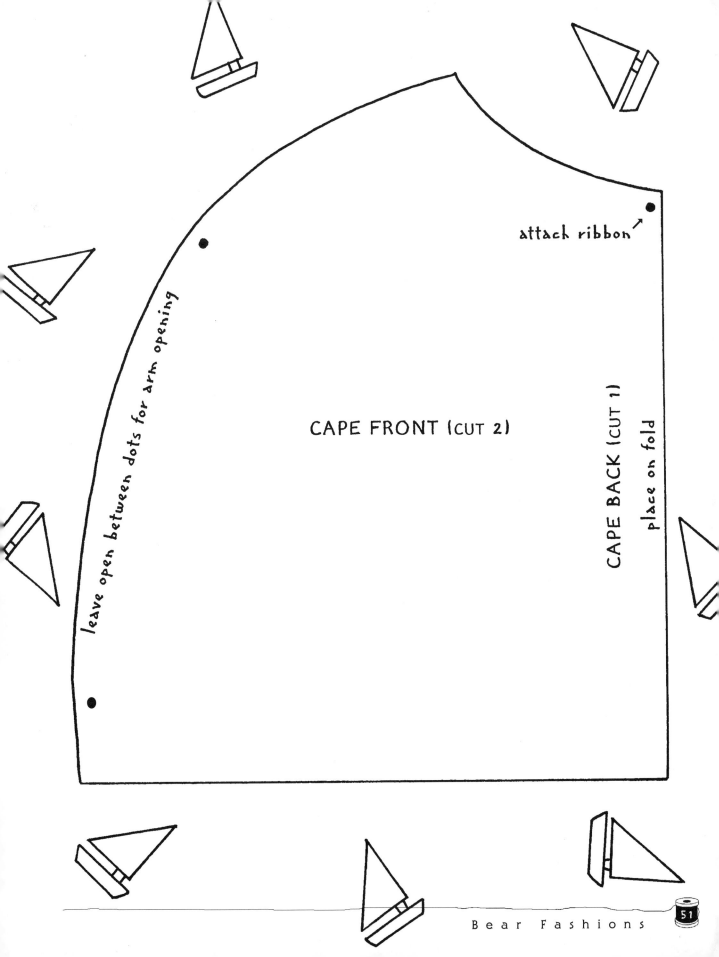

attach ribbon

CAPE FRONT (CUT 2)

leave open between dots for arm opening

CAPE BACK (CUT 1) place on fold

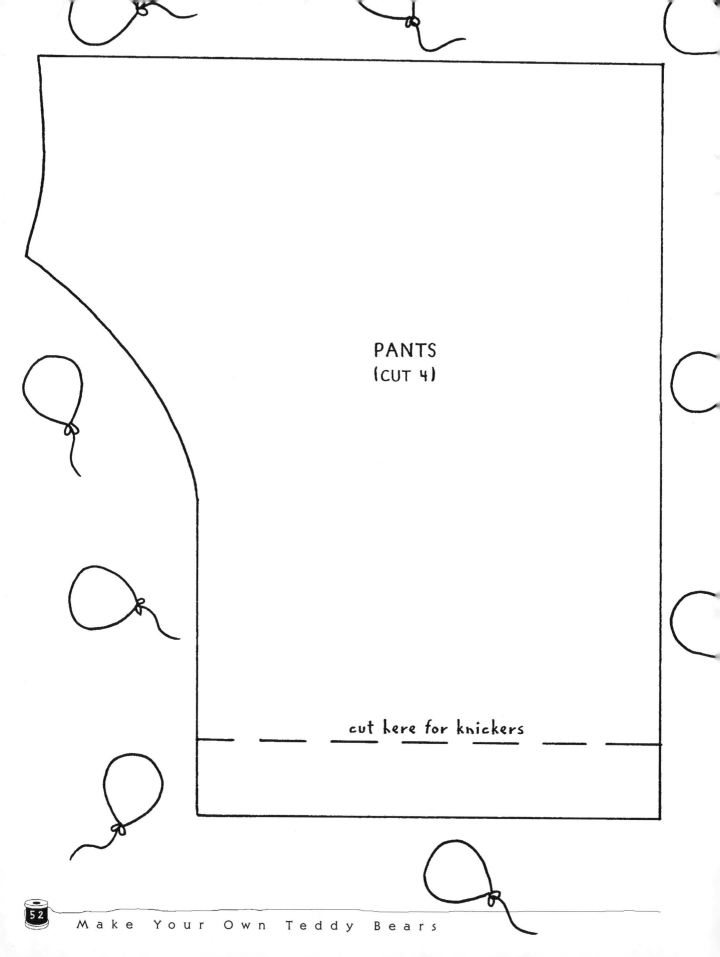

PANTS
(CUT 4)

cut here for knickers

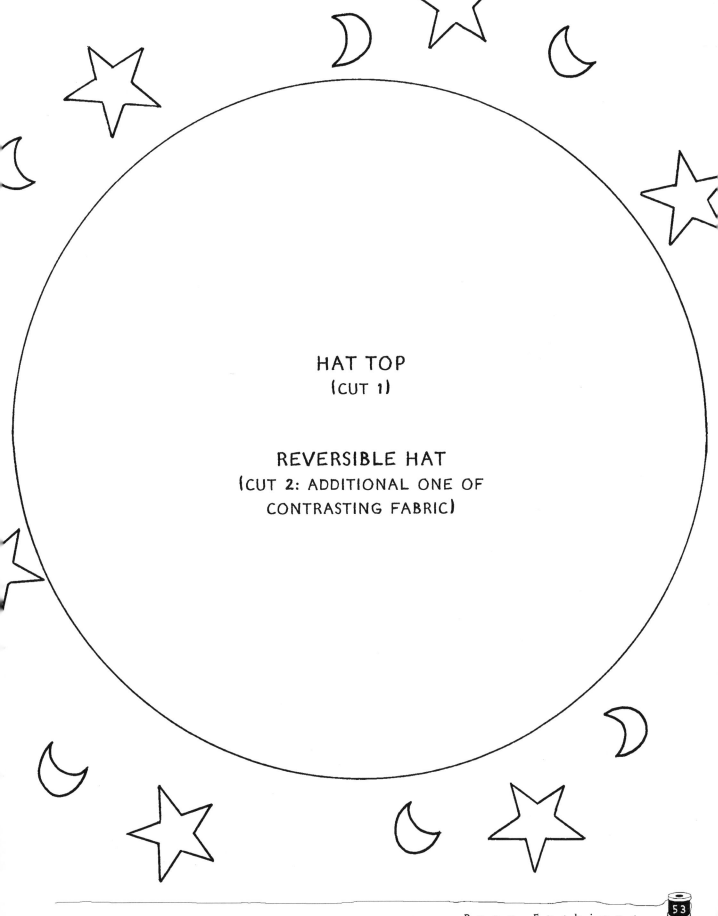

HAT TOP
(CUT 1)

REVERSIBLE HAT
(CUT 2: ADDITIONAL ONE OF
CONTRASTING FABRIC)

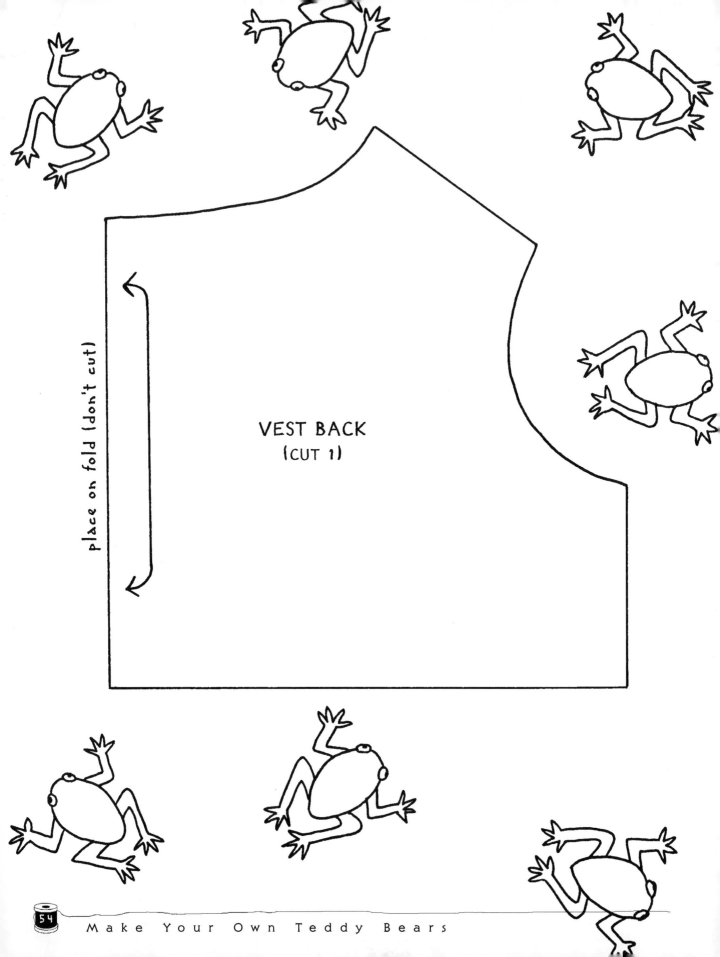

VEST BACK
(CUT 1)

place on fold (don't cut)

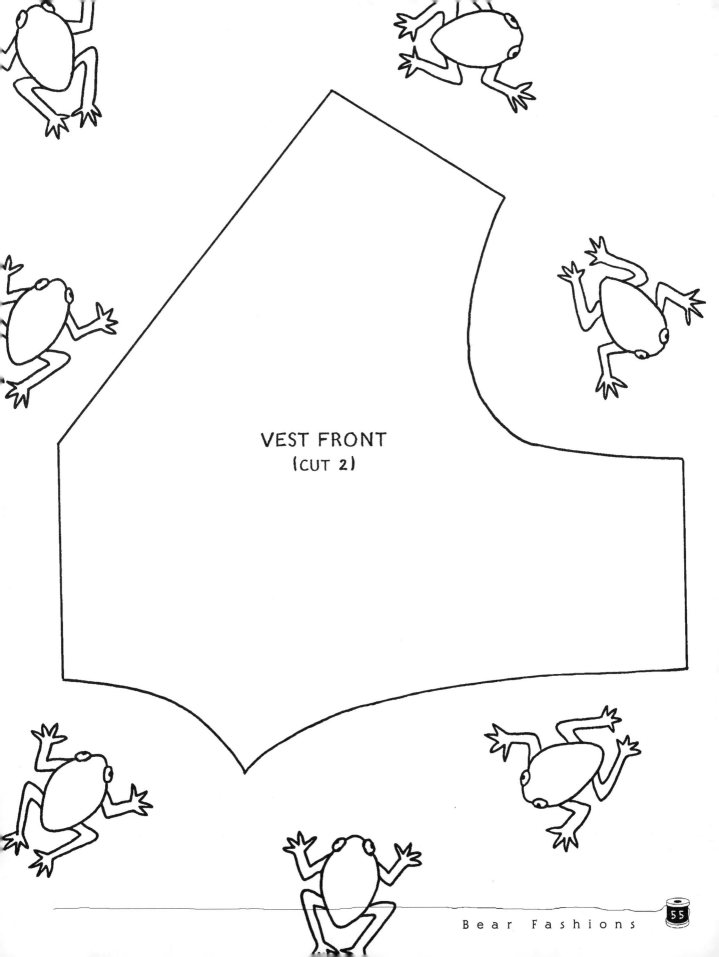

VEST FRONT
(CUT 2)

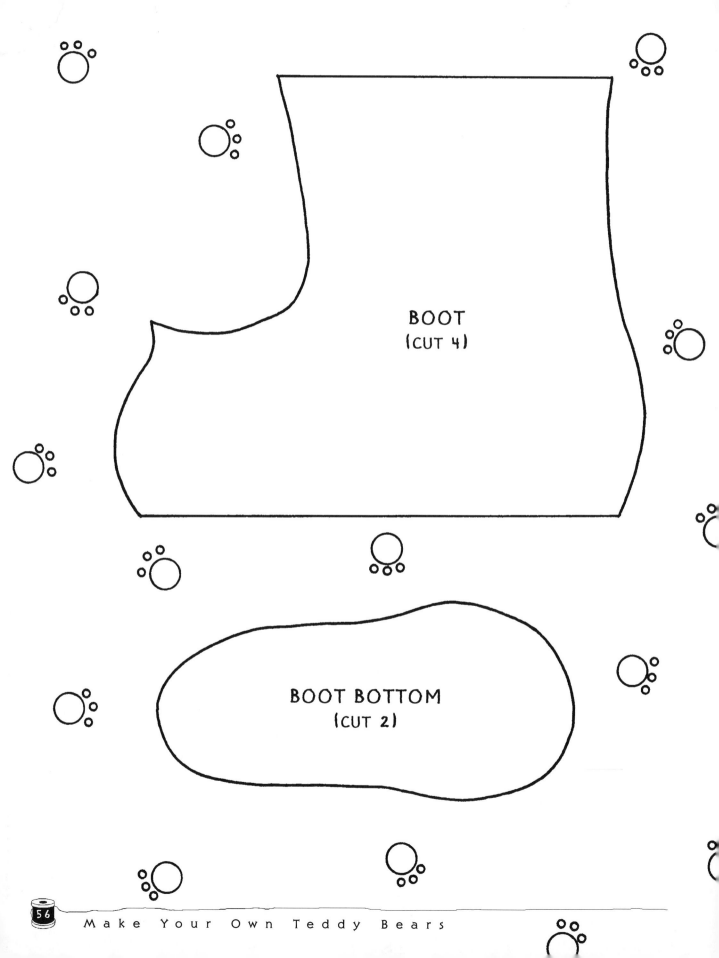

BOOT
(CUT 4)

BOOT BOTTOM
(CUT 2)

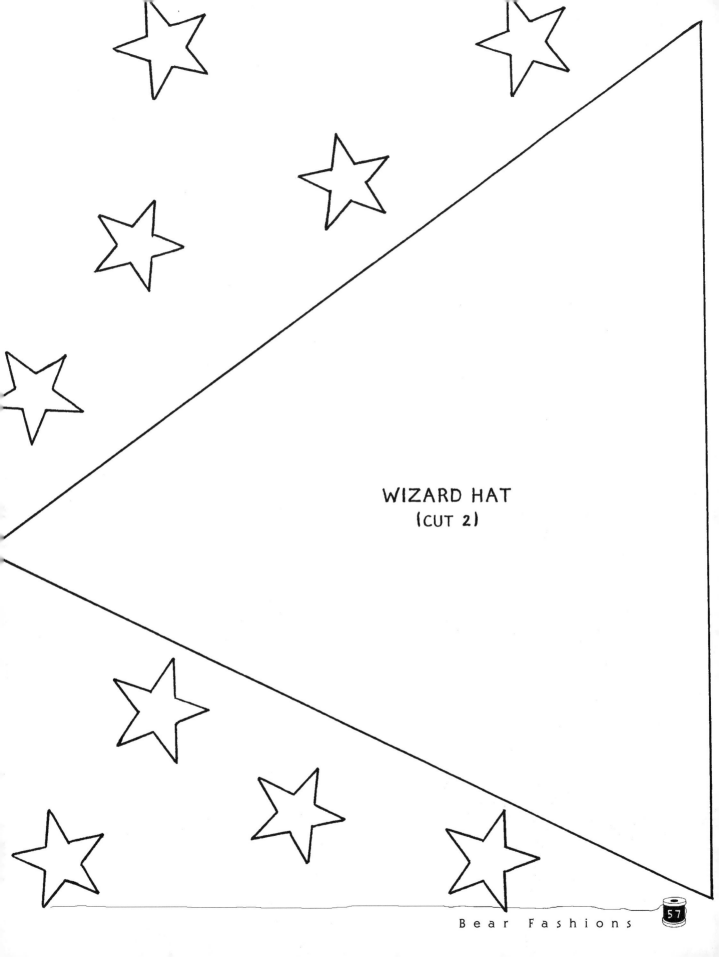

WIZARD HAT
(CUT 2)

APPLIQUÉ
STAR
PATTERN

APPLIQUÉ
MOON
PATTERN

WAND STAR

APPLIQUÉ
SUN
PATTERN

Illustrated Stitch Dictionary & How-to Guide

Appliqué

To *appliqué* means to add some fabric shapes onto the finished craft — such as a felt heart to Little Bear or Big Teddy. If you're appliquéing with felt, you can cut the shape out in the same size you want the finished shape. Then, you can WHIPSTITCH it on with stitches or stick it to the fabric with Velcro stick-on dots. For other fabrics, such as cotton prints, cut the shape a little larger than you want the finished shape to be — about 1/2" (1 cm) larger all around. Then, fold under the edge and pin it onto the fabric. WHIPSTITCH it in place.

Backstitch

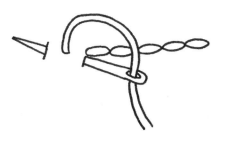

This is a very strong stitch, good for sewing the seams of the bear's body. To start a backstitch, knot the thread and bring needle up through the fabric. Now take a small backward stitch *behind* the thread. Bring the needle up *ahead* of the thread, and pull the thread through. Continue in the same pattern, always starting each stitch *behind* the previous one.

Basting Stitch

This long (at least ¼"/5 mm) stitch is used for holding two pieces of fabric together to make sure they fit properly before you do your final stitching. The ends are not knotted because you'll want to pull the basting stitches out after the final stitching.

Blanket Stitch

This is a great stitch for finishing raw edges in a beautiful design. Knot the thread and bring needle up at A (along the lower line). Insert the needle at B and point it straight down. Come up again at C, this time making sure that the previous thread is *under* the needle. Pull the stitch tight. The thread at C becomes the new A. Insert the needle again at a new B to continue the same pattern.

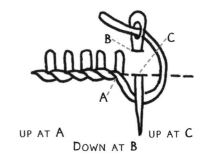

UP AT A   UP AT C

DOWN AT B

Clipping Curves & Corners

Clipping is a handy way to make corners and curved seam allowances lie smoothly when you turn the clothing right side out. Be careful not to clip too close to the seam, though!

- ◎ For *inward curves:* Make little snips in the seam allowance.
- ◎ For *outward curves:* Make little notches.
- ◎ For *corners:* Trim across.

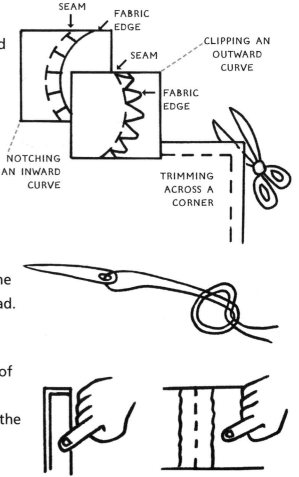

SEAM

FABRIC EDGE

CLIPPING AN OUTWARD CURVE

SEAM

FABRIC EDGE

NOTCHING AN INWARD CURVE

TRIMMING ACROSS A CORNER

Double-Threading the Needle

This just means you thread your needle and knot the two ends together to form a double-stranded thread.

Finger Pressing

You don't need an iron to flatten your fabric most of the time. All you need to do is press your finger down on the side of the seam or down the fold of the fabric to make a temporary crease.

Making a French Knot

French knots are fun and not at all difficult to do. They add a nice decorative look, perfect for tiny buttonlike bumps or miniature eyes. Knot the thread and bring the needle up from the WRONG side to the RIGHT SIDE, just where you want the knot to be. Wrap the thread around the tip of the needle four times, and then insert the needle into the fabric as close as possible to the point where you came up through the fabric. Slowly pull the needle until the thread secures the four little twists. What's left will be a French knot!

Inside Out (See page 15.)

Right Side

For Right Sides Together, Right Sides Out, and Right Sides Down, see page 15.

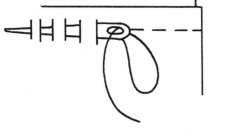

Running Stitch

This stitch is great for making seams. It's similar to the basting stitch, but uses shorter, more even stitches for permanent sewing. It's called the running stitch because the needle and thread "run" through several stitches at once, letting you make stitches in a hurry! To start, knot the thread and bring the needle up through. Work the tip of the needle in and out of the fabric to create three or four stitches and then pull the thread through. Continue in this way until you finish the seam.

Satin Stitch

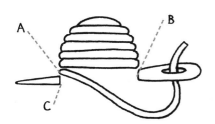

Just as its name suggests, this stitch makes a wonderfully silky look. Use pearl-cotton embroidery floss for best results. Keeping the knotted embroidery floss smooth and flat, bring needle up at A, down at B, and up at C, making long stitches *right next to one another*, hiding the fabric underneath.

Topstitch

The topstitch is sewn onto the finished (RIGHT) side of the fabric. It is used to decorate and secure casings or hems and is often done in a contrasting thread color so that it shows up well.

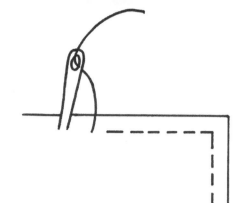

Tracing & Cutting Patterns

- ◎ Using a pencil, trace the pattern onto tracing paper and include all markings.
- ◎ When indicated, tape tracing-paper pieces together to make a whole pattern piece.
- ◎ Using a pencil, trace the paper pattern onto cardboard.
- ◎ Cut out the cardboard pieces.
- ◎ Label each piece with its pattern name and the number of pieces to be cut.
- ◎ When indicated, turn cardboard pieces over and label REVERSE side.

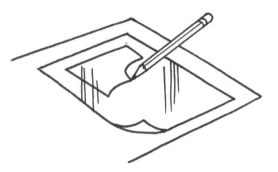

Whipstitch

The whipstitch is used to join two finished edges — such as when closing the turned-under seam on Big Teddy's back or the arm seam of Little Bear. Bring the needle from the WRONG side of the fabric to the RIGHT side to hide the knot in your thread. Now, wrap the thread across the two fabric pieces. Continue wrapping stitches over the seam until the seam is sewn.

Wrong Side   (See page 15.)

INDEX